# BEAKS AND NOSES

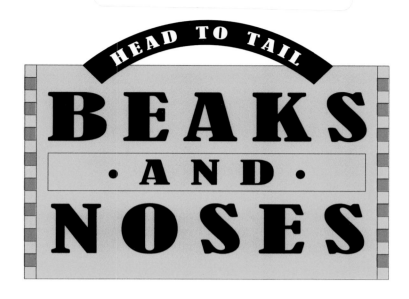

# HEAD TO TAIL
# BEAKS
# · AND ·
# NOSES

WRITTEN BY
THERESA GREENAWAY

SCIENTIFIC CONSULTANT JOYCE POPE
ILLUSTRATED BY
ANN SAVAGE AND HELEN WARD

RSVP®
RAINTREE
STECK-VAUGHN
PUBLISHERS
The Steck-Vaughn Company

Austin, Texas

**Library of Congress Cataloging-in-Publication Data**

Greenaway, Theresa, 1947–
Beaks and noses / by Theresa Greenaway.
p. cm. — (Head to tail)
Includes index.
ISBN 0-8114-8268-5
1. Bill (Anatomy)—Juvenile literature. 2. Nose—Juvenile literature.
3. Animals—Juvenile literature. [1. Bill (Anatomy). 2. Nose. 3. Animals.]
I. Title. II. Series: Greenaway, Theresa, 1947–    Head to tail.
QL697.G74     1995
591.4—dc20
94–29045    CIP    AC

**Editors**: Wendy Madgwick and Kim Merlino
**Designer**: Janie Louise Hunt

Printed in Spain
1 2 3 4 5 6 7 8 9 0 LB 99 98 97 96 95 94

# Contents

# All About Beaks

All birds have beaks. A bird uses its beak in many ways. It uses its beak to pick up food or build a nest. A beak can even give a sharp peck. The shape of a bird's beak can tell you what it eats. A bird that eats fish or mammals has one kind of beak. A bird that eats tiny insects or seeds has a different kind.

▶ **Golden Eagle** This golden eagle eats other animals. It is a bird of prey. An eagle cannot swallow its prey whole. It uses its strong, hooked beak to pull off small bits. Then it swallows the meat.

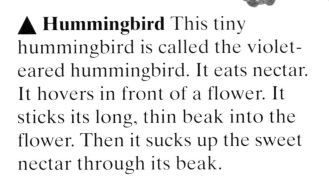

▲ **Hummingbird** This tiny hummingbird is called the violet-eared hummingbird. It eats nectar. It hovers in front of a flower. It sticks its long, thin beak into the flower. Then it sucks up the sweet nectar through its beak.

▼ **Tawny Frogmouth** The speckled brown frogmouth is hard to see in its bush. If an enemy comes close, the frogmouth acts quickly. It opens its beak wide to show its big, pale mouth. This gives the enemy a scare. Then the bird can fly away.

▼ **Sociable Weaver** These sociable weavers help each other at nesting time. The birds pick up bits of grass with their short beaks. They make a big grassy roof. Under the roof, each pair of birds builds its own nest.

▼ **Great Hornbill** The hornbill has a very big curved beak. It uses its beak to reach out for small, ripe berries. It flips a berry into the air. Then it catches the berry and swallows it whole.

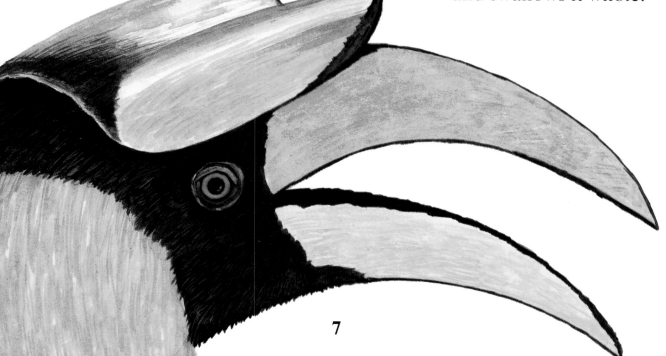

# All About Noses

Noses come in all shapes and sizes. Most animals use their noses to breathe. Look at your nose in a mirror. Keep your mouth shut and breathe in through your nose. The air goes up your nose and down into your lungs. When you breathe out, air goes out through your nose. Animals also use their noses to smell things. Some animals even use their noses to win a mate.

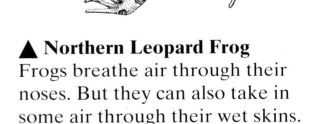

▲ **Northern Leopard Frog** Frogs breathe air through their noses. But they can also take in some air through their wet skins.

▲ **Plains Zebra** The striped zebra is a kind of horse. Horses sniff the air a lot with their soft noses. This is so they can tell when danger is coming.

◀ **African Wild Dog** African wild dogs hunt in packs. Like most dogs, they have good senses of sight and smell. They use their noses to find the scent left by herds of prey animals.

▲ **Proboscis Monkey** A male proboscis monkey has a big, wobbly nose! It is so big that it hangs right over his mouth! It makes the females notice him.

# Crackers

Some animals eat things that are hard to get at. Things like nuts or shellfish have very hard shells. Animals that eat these things often have big strong beaks. They can easily crack open these hard shells. Then they can eat the soft, tasty food inside.

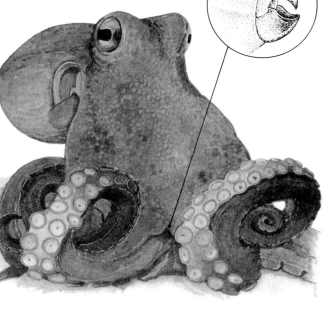

▲ **Blue Parrot Fish** The teeth of the parrot fish are joined together to make a hard beak. The parrot fish uses its beak to break open corals.

▼ **Hawfinch** Finches are small birds that eat seeds as hard as cherry pits. The hawfinch has a short but very strong beak. It can crack open much harder seeds than other finches.

▲ **Common Octopus** The octopus lives at the bottom of the ocean. It catches crabs with its eight long arms. The octopus cracks open crabs with its strong beak. Then it eats them.

▲ **Macaw** The blue and yellow macaw has a very strong beak. It can crack open some of the hardest nuts in the jungle. The macaw can eat nuts that other birds leave behind.

▶ **Eider Duck** The eider duck swims in the sea. It feeds on mussels. It dives down to the ocean floor and pulls off a mussel. It crushes the hard shell with its strong beak. Then it eats the soft flesh.

# Pokers and Probers

Some tasty foods are difficult to reach. They may lie deep in the ground or inside tree trunks. Birds with long, thin beaks can push into these places. They can find this hidden food. They can reach food that birds with short beaks cannot reach. This means different kinds of birds can live close together. They can all find enough to eat.

▼ **Avocet** The avocet has a long thin beak that curves upward. It wades through shallow water. It moves its beak back and forth in the soft mud at the bottom. When it finds a little water animal, the avocet gobbles it up.

▶ **Limpkin** Not many birds can get snails out of their shells. The limpkin can! It holds the snail's shell between its toes. Then it pulls out the snail with its long, strong beak.

**◀ Curlew** This curlew has an even longer beak than the avocet. The curlew's beak curves downward. The curlew sticks its beak deep into soft mud. Here it can search out tiny animals that live in deep burrows.

**▲ Oystercatcher** The oystercatcher can poke the sharp tip of its beak into mussels. It snips up the animal inside and opens the shell. Then it can enjoy its dinner.

**▶ Brown Kiwi** The kiwi lives in New Zealand. It has a long, thin beak. The kiwi finds its food by poking its beak into fallen leaves or soft earth.

# In Touch

Many animals sleep all day and come out at night. Some live in places that are dark all the time. The darkness helps them to hide from enemies. But it is much harder to find food in the dark. These animals often have sensitive noses. They find their food by feeling for it. Sometimes they find food by its smell.

▲ **Star-Nosed Mole** The star-nosed mole looks really weird. All around its nose are soft "fingers." These feel for food as the mole swims along at the bottom of a stream.

▶ **Goblin Shark** The goblin shark's nose is covered in tiny holes. These pick up smells in the water. This means the shark can track animals from a long way off.

**▼ Atlantic Hagfish** The hagfish is eyeless and slimy. It has long feelers around its nose. The hagfish eats dead or dying sea animals. It finds its food by smelling for it.

**▲ American Wood Stork** An American wood stork feeds in muddy water. To find its food, it dips its long beak into the water. When its beak touches a tiny water animal, it snaps shut *very* fast!

**▼ Russian Desman** This Russian desman has a long nose that bends. It uses it to feel for prey at the bottom of streams.

# Super Scoops

Lakes and oceans contain tiny animals and plantlike living things. Some are too small to see. The water containing the animals is something like thin soup. Hungry animals cannot pick out these tiny creatures one by one. They have other ways. Some birds have beaks like big spoons. They scoop up a big mouthful. They let the water drain away. Then they swallow the thousands of tiny animals trapped in their beak.

▼ **Greater Flamingo** The flamingo eats with its head upside down. It sucks in a beakful of lake water and tiny shrimp. The water drains away through fringes along the beak. The tiny shrimp are trapped and swallowed.

▲ **Roseate Spoonbill** The end of a spoonbill's beak is round and flat. This traps small water animals but lets the water run away.

## ▲ Pterodaustro

This amazing pterosaur lived over 100 million years ago. It flew down to shallow swamps to feed. Pterodaustro scooped up beakfuls of soupy swamp water. The water drained away through bristles along its lower jaw.

## ◄ Platypus

Is this a duck or a mole? No, it's neither of these. It is a platypus from Australia. The platypus scoops up sand and small animals with its flat, rubbery snout, or bill. It spits out the sand. Then it takes its food onto land to eat.

## ► Shoveler

The shoveler is a duck that scoops up beakfuls of water and the tiny creatures that are in it. The water runs out through bristles along the sides of its beak.

# Goin' Fishin'

Fish are a very good food. But they are not easy to catch. A fish will dart away if it is in danger. When a fish is caught, it is very hard to hold. A layer of slime over its body makes it slippery. Birds that eat fish have clever ways of catching them. They also have special beaks. These help them catch and hold on to the slippery fish.

▼ **Shoe-Billed Stork** The big beak of the shoe-billed stork looks clumsy. But it is very good at catching fish. The stork grips the fish with the hook on the tip of its beak.

▲ **Black Skimmer** A skimmer has a clever way to catch fish. The bottom part of its beak is much longer than the top. The bird flies low over the ocean with the bottom part of its beak in the water. Little fish near the surface are trapped between the two parts of the beak.

**◀ African Snakebird** This bird dives to hunt for fish. It has a long neck and a very sharp beak. When a fish comes near, the snakebird shoots its neck out. It spears the fish with its sharp beak.

**▼ Red-Breasted Merganser** This merganser makes sure that its prey does not get away. The sides of its beak are like saws. The saw-toothed edges grip the fish that it catches.

**▼ Kingfisher** The kingfisher sits very still above the water. When it sees a fish, it dives into the water. It catches the fish in its beak.

19

# Feeding Time!

Feeding chicks means a lot of work for the parents. They look for food everywhere. When they find it, they carry the food home in their beaks. They also use their beaks to feed their chicks.

▲ **Puffin** The little puffin eats sand eels. It can carry lots of eels in its colorful beak. It holds the fish in the middle. The heads and tails stick out on both sides.

▶ **Swift** A swift catches insects in its beak as it flies. When its mouth is full, the swift flies back to its nest. It feeds the insects to its babies.

**White Pelican** The pelican scoops up fish in its stretchy beak. Then it swallows them whole. Big chicks put their heads right inside the pelican's mouth. They find the fish their parents bring back.

**Blackbird** A blackbird pecks ants, spiders, and grubs. It carries the food back to the nest in its beak. It can then feed its chicks.

**Barn Owl** The barn owl hunts at night. When the owl sees a small animal, it swoops down. It catches its prey in its claws. Then it carries its prey to the nest in its hooked beak.

# Nosing Around

Many animals find their food by sniffing around on the ground. They search in fallen leaves of a forest. They poke around in tufts of grass on a prairie. Or they search for soft grubs in rotten logs. They use their noses to sniff out food.

▶ **Ringtail Coati** A ringtail coati uses its long nose to find things to eat. It can sniff out insects, grubs, and tasty plant roots.

▲ **Giant Elephant Shrew** A giant elephant shrew needs to eat a lot to keep active. It probes for insects, spiders, and grubs with its thin nose.

▶ **Long-Beaked Echidna** This echidna lives on the warm, damp floor of a New Guinea jungle. Its long nose looks a little like a worm! It uses its nose to search in the fallen leaves. The echidna is looking for worms to eat.

## ▲ Eurasian Badger

The badger has a great sense of smell.
It can tell if food is hidden in the ground.
It scratches up the earth with its long claws.
Then it pushes its nose into the soil to find
worms or seeds.

## ▲ Malayan Tapir

The Malayan tapir lives deep
in the jungle. It uses its long
snout, which bends, to sniff
out and eat the best leaves.

# Finding a Mate

Every kind of animal produces young. Some male animals try hard to attract a female mate. They may have special beaks or noses to make a female notice them. The male's beak or nose may be extra large. Sometimes a male's nose is brightly colored or a funny shape. Noses like these look odd to us. But they are useful to the animal.

▼ **Hooded Seal** Male hooded seals have lots of mates. They puff out a big balloon over their nose. Then they puff another, a red balloon, out of their left nostril!

▲ **Andean Condor** The Andean condor has a big floppy, gray wattle on top of his head. It hangs down over his beak. When he sees a female, it turns purplish-pink.

▶ **Common Scoter** Male ducks are called drakes. This common scoter drake has a beak with knobs at the base. He uses it to show off to his mate.

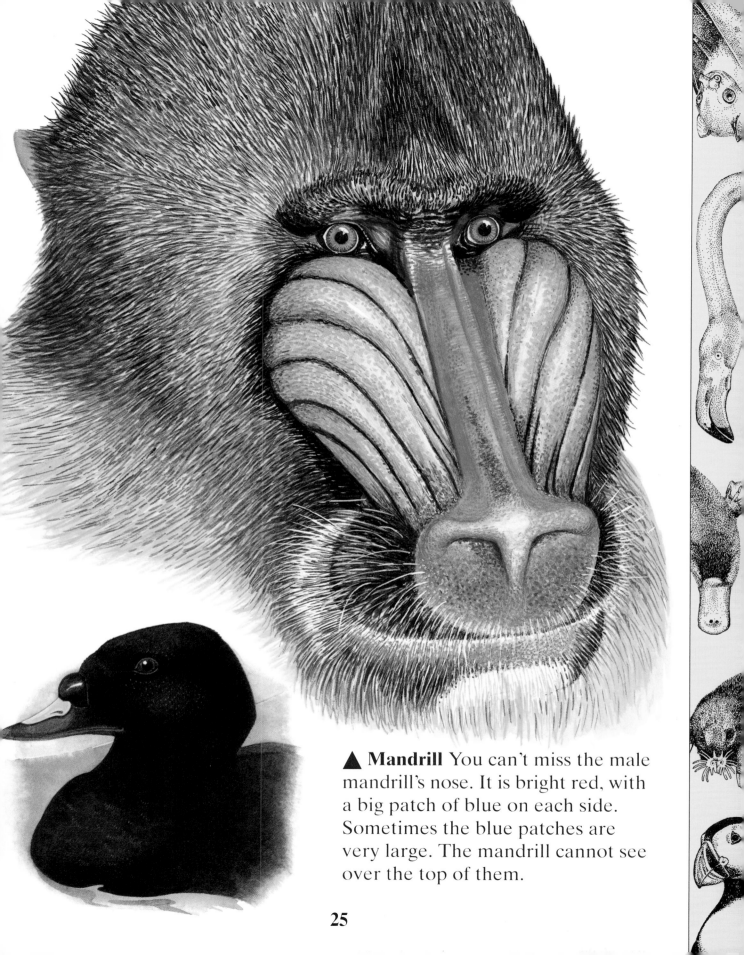

▲ **Mandrill** You can't miss the male mandrill's nose. It is bright red, with a big patch of blue on each side. Sometimes the blue patches are very large. The mandrill cannot see over the top of them.

25

# Which Way?

Some animals live in the dark. They find their way around or find food in special ways. Some make little sounds through their noses or mouths. Often these sounds are too high for most people to hear. The sounds go through the air or water. When they hit something, an echo bounces back. The animal hears the echo. Then it can tell where the object is. Some fish light up their noses. This helps their food find them!

▶ **Oilbird** All day long, the oilbird sleeps in a dark cave. At night, it wakes and flies off to find fruit to eat. It finds its way around the cave by making clicks with its beak. These echo when they hit the cave walls.

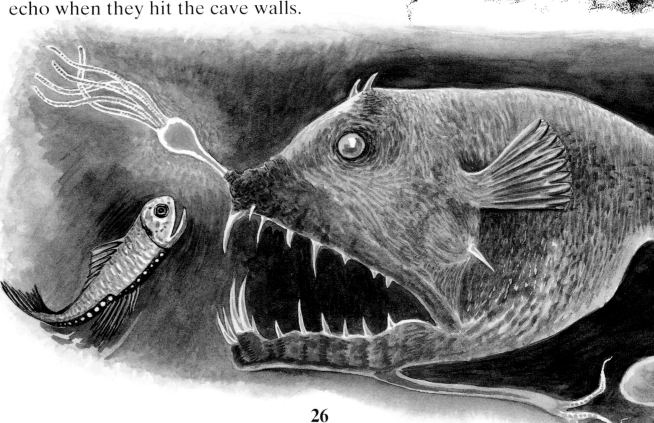

**▼ Greater Horseshoe Bat** The greater horseshoe bat eats big beetles. It makes sounds through flaps on its nose. The sound hits a beetle and bounces back. When the bat hears the echo, it knows where the beetle is.

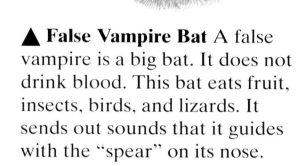

**▲ False Vampire Bat** A false vampire is a big bat. It does not drink blood. This bat eats fruit, insects, birds, and lizards. It sends out sounds that it guides with the "spear" on its nose.

**▼ Deep-Sea Anglerfish** The deep-sea anglerfish dangles a light on the end of its nose! Small creatures swim up to have a closer look. Then — gulp! The anglerfish has a tasty meal.

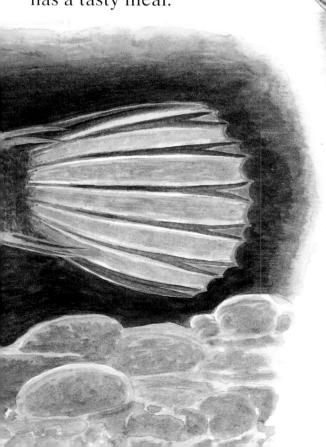

**▲ Yangtze River Dolphin** This river dolphin lives in muddy water. The dolphin finds its way around by making clicks with its beak. There is a special bump of bones just above this beak. These bones pick up the echoes from these sounds.

# Take a Deep Breath

How does an animal breathe if it lives in water? How does a desert animal keep sand from its nose? How do anteaters keep angry insects out of their noses? Not all animals have solved these problems. Those that have live in difficult places. They can also eat food that others cannot.

▼ **Dromedary** Dusty sandstorms happen a lot in hot deserts. The camel closes both of its narrow nostrils to keep out the sand.

▲ **Aardvark** The aardvark eats ants. As soon as it digs into an ant nest, the ants swarm all over it. The aardvark has lots of hairs in its nostrils. These keep the ants from crawling up its nose.

▶ **Matamata** The matamata turtle breathes air. It lies quite still in shallow water waiting for its prey. The matamata's nose turns up and sticks out of the water. This means it can breathe while it waits.

**▶ Sloth Bear** A sloth bear feeds on termites. It breaks open a termite nest and blows away dust and bits of nest. Then the bear sucks up the termites. Its soft, floppy nose closes right up. This keeps the termites from going down the wrong way!

**▲ Fin Whale** A whale's nostrils are no longer on the end of its nose! Instead, air goes in and out through a blowhole on the whale's back. It closes this hole when it swims under the water.

# What a Nose!

Animals have noses that are just right for them. Some have rather large noses. They often look strange or funny to us. We know why some animals are like they are. We do not know why others need such huge noses.

▼ **Northern Elephant Seal** A male northern elephant seal likes his own space on the beach. He roars to tell other males to keep away. He blows up his nose to form a big sac. This makes his roar sound even louder.

▲ **Dugong** The dugong has a big blunt nose. Its nostrils are right on the top. This means it can breathe in air while its body is underwater. The rest of its nose is really a huge upper lip. The dugong uses it to pull up waterweeds.

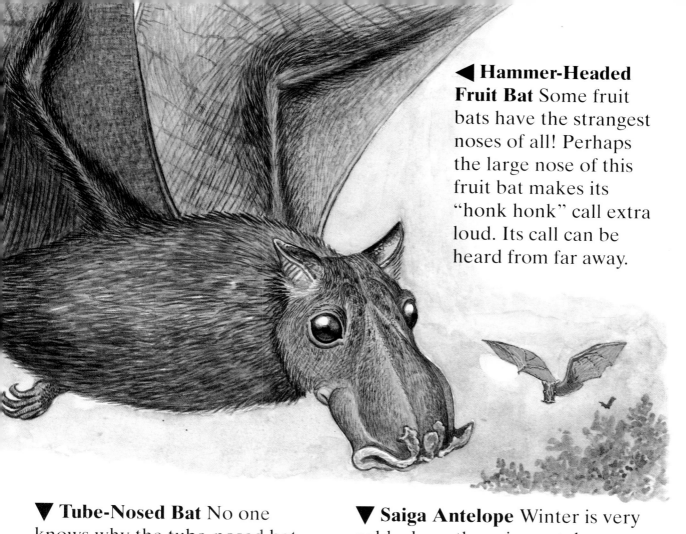

**◄Hammer-Headed Fruit Bat** Some fruit bats have the strangest noses of all! Perhaps the large nose of this fruit bat makes its "honk honk" call extra loud. Its call can be heard from far away.

**▼ Tube-Nosed Bat** No one knows why the tube-nosed bat has a nose like this. It is a bit of a puzzle. Perhaps one day we'll learn why.

**▼ Saiga Antelope** Winter is very cold where the saiga antelope lives. Its big heavy nose warms the air before it reaches the antelope's lungs.

# Biggest is Best

The elephant's trunk is the biggest nose of all. It is about 80 inches (2 m) long. The elephant uses its nose to breathe. It also uses it to smell things. However an elephant's trunk can do much more than this!

▶ **Phiomia** Many other kinds of elephants lived a very long time ago. This Phiomia lived 35 million years ago. It had a short trunk.

▼ **African and Indian Elephants** use their trunks to…

…reach fruits growing high up on a tree.

…move a fallen tree out of their way.

### ◀ Woolly Mammoth

The woolly mammoth was huge and very hairy. Even its long trunk was covered with fur to keep it warm. It lived in the cold lands of the Northern Hemisphere. Although it is extinct, we know just what it looked like. Some of these mammoths have been found frozen in the ice in Siberia.

...have a drink or a refreshing shower.

...pick up food and eat it.

# Quiz

**1. How does the black skimmer catch fish?**

**2. What does a dromedary do in a sand storm?**

**3. What does a hummingbird eat?**

**4. Why does the giant elephant shrew have a long nose?**

**5. Which animals do these beaks belong to?**

**(a)**

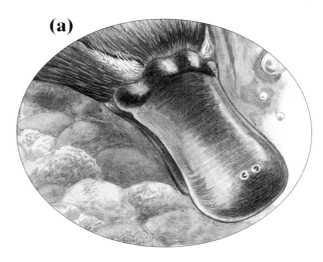

**(b)**

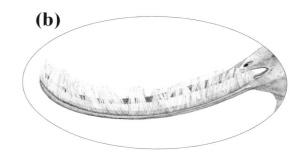

**6. Why does the saiga antelope have a big nose?**

**7. How does the hagfish find its food?**

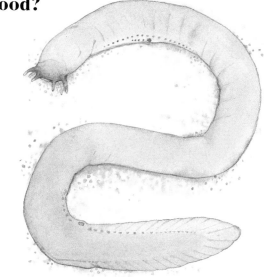

**8. Why does the curlew have a long beak?**

**9. Which animals do these noses belong to?**

**(a)**

**(b)**

**10. How does a frog breathe?**

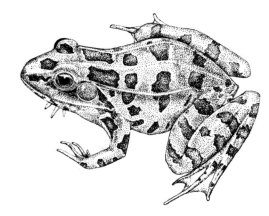

**11. How does the greater horseshoe bat find its food?**

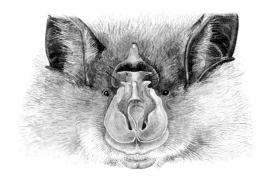

If you do not know the answers turn to the following pages:
**1.** p18, **2.** p28, **3.** p6, **4.** p22, **5a.** p17, **5b.** p17, **6.** p31, **7.** p15, **8.** p13, **9a.** p14, **9b.** p24, **10.** p8, **11.** p27

# Glossary

**Ants** A group of insects that live in nests, or colonies, containing thousands of individuals.

**Berry** A small fruit containing one or more seeds.

**Breathe** To draw air into the lungs and then to push it out.

**Burrow** A large tunnel that many kinds of animals dig in the ground. Some animals live in their burrows. Others just use them to sleep in or to make nests for their young. Sometimes they dig them to find food.

**Chick** A young bird.

**Corals** Tiny sea animals that make a hard chalky skeleton around themselves. The skeletons are joined together to make large underwater coral reefs.

**Echo** A sound that has been bounced off an object.

**Extinct** A kind of living thing that has completely died out.

**Frog** An animal that lives part of its life in water and part of its life on land.

**Herd** A large number of grazing animals that feed and travel around together.

**Insect** A small animal with six legs. The adult has a hard case around its body. Most insects have two or four wings.

**Jungle** A thick forest with plenty of undergrowth.

**Lungs** The parts of the body where air goes when it is breathed in.

**Mate** Each of a pair of animals that gets together to produce young.

**Mussel** A soft-bodied sea animal with a very hard shell made up of two parts.

**Nectar** A sweet, sugary liquid that is made by flowers. Many animals feed on nectar.

**Nest** A special place made and lived in by an animal. Some animals lay their eggs or bring up their young in a nest.

**Nostril** A hole in the animal's nose where the air passes in and out.

**Pack** A group of animals of the same kind that live and hunt together.

**Prairie** Large areas of North America that were once covered with grasslands.

**Predator** An animal that kills and eats other animals.

**Prey** An animal that is killed and eaten by another animal.

**Seeds** Small dry objects produced by flowers. Under the right conditions, seeds will sprout and grow into new plants.

**Shellfish** Many different kinds of soft-bodied sea animals that are encased in a hard, chalky shell.

**Shells** The hard, chalky layer that covers some kinds of soft-bodied animals.

**Termites** A group of antlike insects that live together in enormous colonies in hot climates. They sometimes build large mounds that stick up many feet above ground.

**Wattle** A fleshy, brightly colored piece of loose skin that hangs down from a bird's head or neck.

# Index

**A TEMPLAR BOOK**

Devised and produced by The Templar Company plc
Pippbrook Mill, London Road, Dorking,
Surrey RH4 1JE, Great Britain